# PAPER CUTTING

# NEW CRAFTS

# PAPER CUTTING

## STEWART AND SALLY WALTON

## PHOTOGRAPHY BY PETER WILLIAMS

## LORENZ BOOKS

NEW YORK • LONDON • SYDNEY • BATH

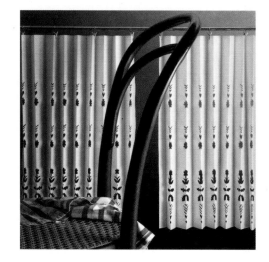

This edition is published in 1997 by Lorenz Books
27 West 20th Street, New York, NY 10011

Lorenz Books are available for bulk purchase
for sales promotion and for premium use. For
details, write or call the manager of special sales:
Lorenz Books, 27 West 20th Street,
New York, New York 10011
(800) 354-9657

Lorenz Books is an imprint of
Anness Publishing Limited

ISBN 1 85967 533 6

Publisher: Joanna Lorenz
Editor: Clare Nicholson
Photographer: Peter Williams
Step-by-Step Photography: Mark Wood
Stylist: Georgina Rhodes
Designer: Roger Walker and Graham Harmer
Illustrators: Madeleine David and Vana Haggerty

Printed and bound in Hong Kong

10 9 8 7 6 5 4 3 2 1

# CONTENTS

# INTRODUCTION

THE BEAUTY OF PAPER CUTTING LIES IN THE SIMPLICITY OF THE CRAFT — YOU ONLY REALLY NEED A SHEET OF PAPER AND A PAIR OF SCISSORS. IN FACT, THE POLISH FOLK ARTISTS, WHO BECAME FAMOUS FOR THE CHARM OF THEIR INTRICATE, COLORFUL PAPER-CUTS, ACTUALLY USED SHEEP SHEARS TO CUT THEM OUT. WE HAVE SUGGESTED USING A COMBINATION OF SMALL, SHARP SCISSORS AND A CRAFT KNIFE FOR THE CUTS IN OUR PROJECTS, AND THERE ARE TOOLS TO SUIT ALL SKILL LEVELS.

THE DISTINCTIVE LOOK OF A SHAPE THAT HAS BEEN CUT OUT RATHER THAN PAINTED, DRAWN OR PRINTED, COMES FROM THE FACT THAT IT HAS AN ABSOLUTE EDGE — NO FUZZY LINES, FADING OR SHADING. ONCE YOU PICK UP THE SCISSORS OR CRAFT KNIFE TO MAKE SOMETHING FROM PAPER, YOU ARE HALFWAY THERE — AND ONCE YOU HAVE TRIED PAPER CUTTING, THERE IS NO GOING BACK.

IN THE INTRODUCTORY SECTION OF THE BOOK WE EXPLORE THE LONG HISTORY OF PAPER CUTTING AND THE WAYS IT HAS BEEN USED IN DIFFERENT CULTURES. THE GALLERY SHOWS A VARIETY OF INTER-PRETATIONS OF THE CRAFT. WE ALSO SHOW USEFUL EQUIPMENT, AND AN ASSORTMENT OF SUITABLE PAPERS, AND EXPLAIN THE SIMPLE TECHNIQUES THAT WILL HELP YOU TO PROGRESS QUICKLY.

*Opposite: Paper cutting produces a wonderfully wide range of results, depending upon the type of paper used, the number of times it is folded, the skill of the cutter and the delicacy or robustness of the design.*

# HISTORY OF PAPER CUTTING

PAPER WAS INVENTED BY THE CHINESE IN THE 2ND CENTURY BC, AND THE KNOWLEDGE OF HOW IT WAS MADE PASSED FROM THE ARABS TO EUROPE MANY CENTURIES LATER. IN CHINA, THE FIRST PAPERCUTS WERE MADE AS PATTERNS TO TRANSFER EMBROIDERY PATTERNS. PEOPLE BEGAN TO APPRECIATE THE INTRINSIC BEAUTY OF THE PAPERCUT, AND PAPER CUTTING DEVELOPED AS A FOLK ART IN ITS OWN RIGHT. UP TO FIFTY LAYERS OF FINE PAPER WOULD BE PLACED IN A FRAME AND CUT OUT AS A BLOCK, USING A VERY SHARP KNIFE. THE IMAGES ON PRESENT-DAY CHINESE PAPERCUTS ARE TRADITIONAL, BUT THESE DAYS THEY ARE MORE LIKELY TO BE CUT BY MACHINE. IN JAPAN, PAPER CUTTING TOOK THE FORM OF STENCILS THAT WERE USED TO PRINT TEXTILES.

Paper cutting came to European folk art via the trade routes from the Far East through the Middle East and Turkey, where the craft was very popular. Paper itself was a rare commodity and was found mostly in monasteries, where monks incorporated paper cutting into their illuminated manuscripts. A lot of early European paper cutting featured religious subjects, but as paper became more freely available, people began to make papercuts that illustrated everyday life.

The Germans and Swiss made very complicated folded papercuts called "*Scherenschnitte*." These are the famous symmetrical black on white images that were taken up as a popular craft by the communities that settled on the eastern coast of America. Some of the loveliest of these are the valentines and love letters that featured hearts, flowers, birds, animals and often words as well. Many of the settlers were fleeing religious persecution in Europe and set up strong communities that kept the crafts of their homelands alive. Some of the communities, such as the Amish and Mennonites, still exist and continue their way of life today, and there are fine examples of paper cuttings in their museums and publications.

Another style of paper cutting, the silhouette portrait, was popular in Britain and France before cameras could capture a likeness in an instant, and most well-to-do families displayed silhouette portraits in their homes. These were the days when ladies spent hours each day doing embroidery and found that

*Above: The famous Danish author of fairy tales, Hans Christian Andersen, was devoted to the craft of paper cutting. This old book contains printed images of some of his favorite papercuts, which are often quite simple and rustic.*

*Right: In Denmark, people herald the arrival of the first snowdrops in February by sending each other papercuts that are folded and intricately cut with a solid block in the middle to hold a cryptic inscription. The recipient has to guess the identity of the sender — or give them a chocolate egg. This one was made by a fourteen-year-old girl for her godmother.*

their tiny scissors could be used to make papercuts as well — they made delicate lacy love letters, birth certificates and pictures to commemorate engagements and weddings.

Paper cutting did not die out completely in Europe, and there are places where it is still positively thriving. In Denmark, for instance, people send each other cryptic papercuts when the first snowdrops flower in February — the recipient has to guess the identity of the sender or pay up with a chocolate egg! Denmark's most famous author of fairy tales, Hans Christian Andersen, delighted in paper cutting, and many examples of his cuts can be seen in books about him.

Another country where paper cutting has become part of a popular celebration is Mexico where, on the Day of the Dead, people buy large, vibrantly colored papercut pictures, banners and decorations to parade and then burn in the festival. In America people decorate their homes and streets with paper chains cut into the shapes of pumpkins, witches and skulls at Halloween, and in nursery schools children still make paper dolls, chains and decorations at Christmas.

There was a time, when machines and mass production were new, when handmade came to mean hard up, but thankfully that time has passed and attitudes have come full circle. Understanding how easily decorative goods can be churned out by factories has made us value the time and care involved and the unique aesthetic quality of handmade crafts.

*Below: The birth record of Peter Gottschalk, which dates from 1769. Decorative paper cutwork of the early date of this birth record are rare.*

# GALLERY

P APER CUTTING IS A UNIVERSAL ART AND CRAFT THAT IS PRAC-
TICED ALL OVER THE WORLD. IN THIS GALLERY THERE ARE A
SELECTION OF PAPERCUTS USING A WIDE RANGE OF MOTIFS THAT
TAKE THEIR INSPIRATION FROM MANY DIFFERENT CULTURES —
MEXICO, CHINA, THE UNITED STATES AND EUROPE. WHEN YOU HAVE
TACKLED SOME OF THE PROJECTS IN THE BOOK, TAKE INSPIRATION
FROM THE MOTIFS AND TECHNIQUES ILLUSTRATED IN THE GALLERY
AND APPLY THEM TO YOUR OWN DESIGNS.

*Left:* CUTWORK
PICTURE
In this intriguing
picture, the parade of
separate silhouette
figures is framed by an
elaborate arbor
carefully cut out from
a single-folded sheet
to create a mirror
image. To better
appreciate the
intricate technique,
see how many birds
you can find!
ABBY ALDRICH
ROCKEFELLER FOLK
ART CENTER

*Left:* PAPERCUT SCREEN
This screen was inspired by traditional Polish papercuts made at certain times of the year, such as Easter, to decorate farmhouse walls. The papercuts are nicely set off by the cool Scandinavian colors that have been used on the background of the screen, rather than the more exuberant Polish colors.
DEBORAH SCHNEEBELI-MORRELL

*Left:* LOVE TOKEN
The cut and folded paper love token originated in Switzerland and Germany. Skilled papercutters elevated this from a pastime to a skilled craft, creating beautiful symmetrical compositions. This charming love token of two parasoled ladies was cut by the author.
STEWART WALTON

*Above:* CHRISTMAS CARD
This papercut was made using the very latest paper-cutting techniques. The image was designed on computer and then cut by laser into a high-quality black paper.
METRO MODELS

*Right:* CHINESE
PAPERCUTS
Chinese papercuts,
like these, are cut from
compacted paper
blocks – as many as
fifty at a time – then
peeled off and hand-
colored. The subject
matter here is typical:
insects, birds, flowers
and traditional
Chinese motifs such as
the lion dog.
CHINA

*Left and far left:* MEXICAN
PAPERCUTS
Papercuts are widely used in
Mexico as decoration for festive
occasions. They come in a wide
range of colors and depict
traditional images. White
papercuts, such as these two,
are used specifically for
weddings.
MEXIQUE

*Left:* LAMPSHADE
The pineapple used to be a symbol of hospitality and was used in many areas of house decoration by our ancestors. American folk artists simplified the shape into stencil designs, and this paper lampshade blends the style of the stencil with the popular folk art of partial cutting and lifting, to produce a surface texture. At night, when the lamp is lit, the pineapple shape and texture are revealed.
STEWART WALTON

# BASIC TECHNIQUES

PAPER CUTTING IS NOT A COMPLICATED CRAFT, BUT SOME PRACTICE WILL IMPROVE YOUR CUTTING AND FOLDING TECHNIQUE AND HELP YOU TO PRODUCE A NEATER RESULT. HAVING THE RIGHT EQUIPMENT IS IMPORTANT — ESPECIALLY A SHARP PAIR OF SCISSORS OR A CRAFT KNIFE WITH A SUPPLY OF NEW BLADES. SOME PEOPLE PREFER TO CUT WITH SCISSORS, WHILE OTHERS FIND THAT THEY ARE MORE COMFORTABLE WITH A CRAFT KNIFE. YOU NEED TO EXPERIMENT WITH BOTH TO FIND OUT WHICH SUITS YOU BETTER.

## FOLDING PAPER

The number of times you fold the paper will affect how many times the cutout image is reproduced. If you fold once, you get a mirror image, twice, and you get four images, and so on. The Doily and Snowflakes projects make use of more complicated folds, using a protractor to mark off the angles. This means that a number of identical cuts will radiate out from a central point.

## Making a single fold

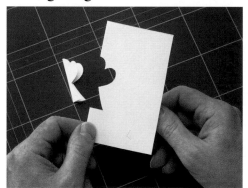

1 Fold the paper in half. Draw half of your pattern on the fold and cut it out.

2 You will have a perfectly symmetrical cutout shape in the middle of the paper.

## Making a double fold

1 Fold a sheet of paper in half, then in half again. Cut a shape out of the middle of the square, not touching any fold or edge.

2 Open out, and you have a shape cut out of each section. Note that each one is facing toward the corner of its square.

## Accordion folds

It is important to measure the first fold accurately and keep the other folds the same size. Check that the right angles remain square.

## Folding by hand

If you want a crisp edge, fold the paper loosely, then run your nail along the crease.

## Folding with thumbnail and ruler

Hold a metal ruler firmly and fold the paper up to its edge and run your nail along it.

## Using a bone paper folder

Bone paper folders are bookbinding tools that give a very crisp edge. Fold the paper loosely, then run the edge of the bone folder along it.

## TRANSFERRING PATTERNS

Patterns have been given for most of the projects. To transfer these to your paper, you can use either a photocopier or tracing paper.

### Photocopying patterns

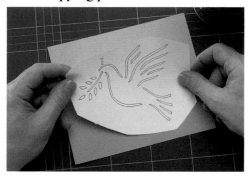

**1** Photocopy the pattern from the back of the book, enlarging it if desired. Cut it out roughly. Spray the back of the copy with spray adhesive and stick it down on the paper that is to be used for the papercut.

**2** Carefully cut out the design, following the lines of the pattern.

**3** When the cutting is complete, remove the photocopy.

### Tracing patterns

Trace the pattern using a pencil. Place the tracing, pencil-side down, on your paper. Rub over the tracing so that the pattern is transferred. Remove the tracing paper and draw over the lines of the pattern.

## CUTTING PAPER

Scissors come in a variety of shapes and sizes. When you are cutting paper always turn the paper toward the blades, keeping them in the most comfortable and controllable position.

### Making internal cuts with scissors

To start an internal cut, poke the sharp ends of the scissors into the center of the paper that is to be removed. Do this in a controlled, careful way, then you can withdraw the scissors and insert the lower blade to cut out the shape with the scissors.

### Using a craft knife

Always work with a cutting mat to protect your work surface and prevent the paper from slipping. Hold the knife like a pencil. If the blade is sharp enough, you should not need to press down hard.

## FINISHING
### Flattening the papercuts

The folds that you have made to reproduce the pattern of your papercut will still be visible after you unfold the finished work. You can flatten it by placing it inside a book and applying pressure with a heavy weight for a day or two. Alternatively, cover the papercut with a sheet of paper and smooth the surface with a small steel ruler or the back of a spoon.

### Protecting your papercuts

A completed papercut can be protected by folding it inside a sheet of paper.

# EQUIPMENT

W E HAVE USED A SELECTION OF DIFFERENT CUTTING AND MEASURING EQUIPMENT TO MAKE THE PROJECTS IN THIS BOOK. THE ESSENTIALS ARE A SHARP PAIR OF SCISSORS AND A SHEET OF PAPER, BUT WITH A FEW EXTRAS YOU CAN EXPAND YOUR PAPER-CUTTING REPERTOIRE AND MASTER ALL ASPECTS OF THE CRAFT. WITH THESE SIMPLE TOOLS, YOU CAN MAKE EVERYTHING FROM VERY SIMPLE FOLK IMAGES TO THE MOST ELABORATE AND COMPLICATED CUTS.

**A bone paper folder** is specifically used on paper to make a crisp edge (see Basic Techniques). Although very useful, this tool is not strictly essential. As an alternative, you could use a metal ruler.

**A fine line black felt-tip marker** makes a clear outline when tracing the patterns at the back of the book.

**Pencils** with hard and soft lead are needed for drawing shapes and transferring tracings. Soft pencils are best for transferring tracings.

**A craft knife** is needed for cutting out detailed inner areas. It can be uncomfortable if you grip it tightly, so bind the shaft with masking tape to make a pad that will be easier to hold. You must change the blade of your craft knife quite frequently, otherwise you will be working with a blunt blade that will catch and snag the paper. A sharp blade will give good, clean cuts. When cutting with a craft knife, always work on a cutting mat to prevent the blade from slipping.

**Pinking shears** are a lot of fun because they give a decorative zigzag edge to papercuts. You can also get scissors with wavy and other decorative edges.

**Scissors** in various sizes are of course one of the main tools of paper cutting. You will need two or three pairs with different sizes of blade for tackling large and detailed projects. When cutting out delicate and intricate shapes, you should use a small pair of scissors, which will give you greater control.

**A spoon** is useful for smoothing over the back of cutouts to remove the folds (see Basic Techniques).

**A revolving hole punch** adjusts to six or more different-size holes. It is ideal for making a row of evenly spaced holes for borders.

**A metal ruler** is needed for cutting straight lines with a craft knife. If you use a clear plastic ruler, your craft knife will snag on the plastic and the straight edge will soon become too messy to work with. You can also tear paper against the sharp edge of a metal ruler (see Basic Techniques).

**A triangle** with 60° and 30° corners enables you to accurately divide circles into sixths.

**A clear plastic ruler** is useful if you need to see the template underneath when you are cutting, such as with the clock face numerals of the Star Clock.

**A protractor** enables you to divide circles into angles.

**A compass** is useful for drawing accurate circles, and it marks the center of the circle at the same time. If you do not have a compass, round objects that you find around the home are good substitutes — for example, plates.

**A cutting mat** is needed when you are using a craft knife. It protects your work surface, and protects you because it prevents the knife from slipping. A cutting mat is self-healing, so it can be used over and over again. The surface of the mat is divided into vertical and horizontal lines to make it easier to check right angles and measurements.

## KEY

| | |
|---|---|
| **1** Bone paper folder | shapes |
| **2** Fine line black felt-tip marker | **9** Small scissors with short, very pointed blades |
| **3** Pencil | **10** Spoon to smooth and flatten folded paper |
| **4** Craft knife | **11** Revolving hole punch |
| **5** Pinking shears | **12** Metal ruler |
| **6** Medium-size scissors for cutting out large shapes | **13** Triangle |
| | **14** Clear plastic ruler |
| **7** Small scissors with medium-length blades | **15** Small steel ruler |
| | **16** Protractor |
| **8** Small scissors with small blades for cutting out intricate | **17** Compass |
| | **18** Cutting mat |

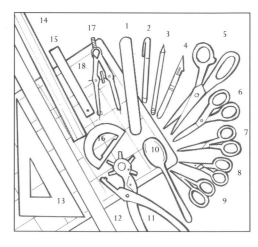

# MATERIALS

PAPER IS, OF COURSE, THE ESSENTIAL MATERIAL IN PAPER CUT-
TING. THERE ARE MANY DIFFERENT TYPES OF PAPER THAT ARE
SUITABLE FOR PAPER CUTTING AND YOU WILL SOON FIND YOUR OWN
PREFERENCES. THE MAIN CONSIDERATION SHOULD ALWAYS BE THE
WEIGHT OF THE PAPER — IF IT IS TOO HEAVY AND THICK IT WILL NOT
FOLD AND CUT WELL. A THIN PIECE OF PAPER CAN STILL BE CUT OUT
BY PLACING IT INSIDE A FOLDED SHEET OF THICKER PAPER AND CUT-
TING THEM BOTH TOGETHER, BUT GREAT CARE MUST BE TAKEN WHEN
HANDLING THE RESULTING PAPERCUT. A VISIT TO A PAPER SPECIALIST
WILL BE WORTHWHILE.

Most papers are made from wood pulp, although there are some that contain a high proportion of fabrics such as linen and cotton. A lot of paper imported from the Far East is made from tropical plants, such as banana, rice and jute, and they often have visible shreds of plant fibers. In India they make a lot of rag paper from recycled clothes — it is high-quality and exceptionally strong. The thinner versions of these papers add an additional dimension of texture to the papercuts. Wood pulp needs to be chemically treated to remove the naturally occurring acids. This weakens the paper and causes instability of color and lack of strength.

The cheapest paper is newsprint. It also happens to be good paper to cut. It creases and folds really well and scissors glide through it. Bond paper is basically wood pulp that has a glue added to bond it together. This is the usual paper for stationery and is also a good paper-cutting material. Laid paper can be identified by the parallel lines that run through it. This is also a stationery paper; it comes in a range of light colors and is suitable for paper cutting. Woven paper is made with a mesh of fine fibers that you can both feel and see. Coated papers may have a color added to one side only — as in the brightly colored or metallic-finish wrapping paper that is currently popular. Experiment with this type of paper before committing yourself to a complex project — the surface color can crack along the fold, which will spoil the outcome of your work.

**Brightly colored craft papers** are available at toy and hobby stores. They are sold in packages and are pre-gummed for a quick lick and stick, although you should use spray adhesive for any sticking. The papers fold and cut with ease.

**Handmade Indian papers** with visible wood chippings and plant fibers are lightweight but strong and easy to cut. Folding depends upon the "bits" that get in the way of a crease.

**Colored craft paper** has strong solid color and is easy to work with if the project only requires one or two folds. It cuts crisply.

**Colored laid paper** is suitable for using in a photocopier. This paper is crisp and folds and cuts very well. It was used for the Bookmarks.

**Crepe paper** is crinkly and stretchy. It comes in lots of bright colors and is widely available at art and hobby stores.

**High-quality tissue paper** has a sheen and is quite strong but very thin. It is great paper to cut and can be folded many times over and still be thin enough for accurate cutting.

**Handmade Japanese papers** are softer to touch than Indian papers but very strong, as they contain long threads of fiber. You can buy them at specialty stores, and they are expensive but worth the money. They cut well but folding is difficult, as they spring back.

**Foil-coated metallic paper** is often coated cellophane paper. It has a tendency to slip and slide and may tear as well. It is, however, the only type to use for real reflective shimmer. Some metallic papers fold well but others are reluctant to unfold once creased. You can buy them as wrapping paper at art stores.

**Glassine paper** is a glazed, colored, heavy tissue-type paper that is mottled and transparent when held up to the light. It folds and cuts beautifully. Get it at a specialty paper dealer or some art stores.

**Coated packing paper** is the familiar brown packing paper dressed up with a coating of silver (or other color) on one or two sides. It is a popular wrapping paper and cuts and folds very well.

**KEY**

| | | | |
|---|---|---|---|
| 1 | Brightly colored craft papers | 6 | Tissue paper |
| 2 | Handmade Indian papers | 7 | Handmade Japanese papers |
| 3 | Colored craft paper | 8 | Foil-coated, metallic and reflective papers |
| 4 | Photocopies on colored laid paper | 9 | Glassine paper |
| 5 | Crepe paper | 10 | Coated packing paper |

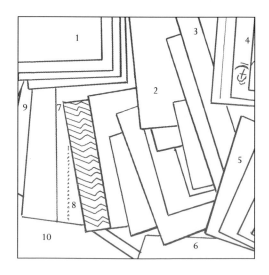

# DECORATED LAMPSHADE

THIS IS A VERY SIMPLE BUT EFFECTIVE WAY TO DECORATE A PLAIN LAMPSHADE. WE HAVE USED NATURAL COLORS, BUT THE PAPER AND SHADE COULD BE BRIGHT OR CONTRASTING IF YOU PREFER — THE METHOD IS THE SAME. THERE ARE THREE DIFFERENT PATTERNS TO TRACE (SEE BASIC TECHNIQUES) AND AN INFINITE NUMBER TO INVENT FOR YOURSELF.

**1** Draw a circle of paper with a 3-inch diameter and cut it out.

**2** Fold the circle in half and make a firm crease with your finger.

**3** Fold the circle in half again and crease firmly with your finger.

**4** Fold in half again. Make a tracing of the patterns at the back of the book, then transfer one of them to the folded paper.

**5** Cut out the edge pattern first. Then do the smaller cuts with a craft knife.

**6** Open out the papercut. Make several more papercuts, then stick the shapes onto the lampshade at regular intervals.

MATERIALS AND EQUIPMENT YOU WILL NEED

THIN PAPER • COMPASS • PENCIL • SCISSORS • TRACING PAPER • CRAFT KNIFE •
CUTTING MAT • PLAIN LAMPSHADE • GLUE STICK OR SPRAY ADHESIVE

# CHINESE LANTERNS

THERE WAS A TIME WHEN ALL CHILDREN SPENT THE WEEKS BEFORE CHRISTMAS CUTTING AND STICKING TOGETHER LENGTHS OF PAPER CHAINS AND PRETTY CHINESE LANTERNS LIKE THESE. THE COLORS USED HERE WILL ADD A TOUCH OF FIESTA TO YOUR CHRISTMAS TREE, ESPECIALLY WHEN LIT BY STRATEGICALLY PLACED TREE LIGHTS. THIS PROJECT CAN INVOLVE THE ENTIRE FAMILY, AND THE LANTERNS WOULD ALSO LOOK LOVELY AT A SUMMER GARDEN PARTY.

**SMALL LANTERNS**

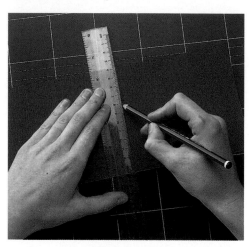

1 For each small lantern, draw a rectangle of crepe paper 5 inches x 4¾ inches. Cut out.

3 Mark another fold 1 inch from the first fold. Cut through the paper up to the guideline. The cuts can be widely or closely spaced to give different effects.

5 Cut the top fold into triangles or decorative fringing.

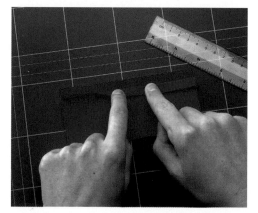

2 Fold in half lengthwise, then fold down ½ inch from both of the top edges.

4 Cut little notches, to add decoration, as shown.

MATERIALS AND EQUIPMENT YOU WILL NEED

DOUBLE-SIDED CREPE PAPER, IN TWO COLORS • RULER • PENCIL • SHARP SCISSORS • GLUE STICK •
CLOTHESPINS • CHRISTMAS TREE LIGHTS • REVOLVING HOLE PUNCH

## LARGE LANTERNS

6 Open the lantern and attach the short sides with the glue stick. Hold together with clothespins until dry.

1 To make a large lantern, cut a 10 x 9-inch rectangle out of crepe paper and fold it in half lengthwise. Fold down a top strip, as you did for the small lantern, then make a second fold 2 inches in from the first fold.

3 Cut slits up to the edge of the added paper, along the whole length of the paper to the second fold.

7 Cut a strip of paper to hang over each light bulb on the tree lights, so that the bulb hangs inside the lantern.

2 Cut two strips in a contrasting color the same length but only 4 inches deep. Fold them in half, then stick each contrasting strip just underneath the folded top edge on either side.

4 Cut decorative notches along the fold edges between the slits.

▶

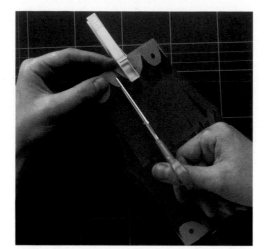

**5** Scallop the edges of the two colored strips, one at a time.

**7** Unfold the lantern, then attach the edges together using the glue stick. Snip the scalloped fringing where the glued edges meet so that you can push out the decorative fringing. Hold together with a clothespin until dry. Add a little strip of paper to hang it up, as you did for the small lantern.

**6** Use the hole punch to make a hole in each scallop shape to reveal the color below.

# PAPER CAFÉ CURTAIN

THIS IS A CLEVER AND VERY ATTRACTIVE WAY TO OBSCURE A WINDOW THAT IS OVERLOOKED, WITHOUT CUTTING OUT THE LIGHT COMPLETELY. THE PAPER NEEDS TO BE QUITE HIGH-QUALITY SO THAT IT WILL NOT CRACK, AND STIFF SO THAT IT WILL HOLD CREASES WELL AND NOT RIP TOO EASILY. VISIT A SPECIALTY PAPER STORE WHERE YOU WILL BE STRUCK BY THE VARIETY OF PAPERS THAT ARE AVAILABLE TODAY — SOME ARE VERY EXPENSIVE BUT OTHERS THAT LOOK SIMILAR ARE VERY REASONABLY PRICED.

1 Measure the window to ascertain how many sheets of paper you will need. Remember that the sheet will be half the width once folded. Use the blunt edge of your scissors to score fold lines of equal width along the length of the paper. The width of the pleats can be that of the ruler, as this is an easy way to make sure they are all the same size.

2 Trace the design from the back of the book, and transfer one half of the pattern onto a strip of cardboard, enlarging if necessary (see Basic Techniques). Slip it under the pleats and lightly trace the pattern along the fold lines.

3 Using sharp scissors, cut out the pattern along the fold lines. To hang the curtain you can either make holes with a hole punch and run a thread along the top, or buy curtain clips that fasten to the top of the paper curtain.

MATERIALS AND EQUIPMENT YOU WILL NEED
PAPER • SCISSORS • RULER • TRACING PAPER • PENCIL • CARDBOARD • REVOLVING HOLE PUNCH

# MEXICAN PAPERCUT BUNTING

MEXICAN PAPERCUTS ARE TRADITIONALLY MADE FROM BRIGHTLY COLORED TISSUE PAPER. THESE ONES ARE CUT FROM STRONG TRANSLUCENT GLASSINE PAPER, BUT YOU CAN USE ANY BRIGHTLY COLORED LIGHTWEIGHT PAPER CHOSEN FROM THE HUNDREDS OF KINDS AVAILABLE. THE FINISHED PAPERCUT CAN BE HUNG UP AS DECORATION AT A WINDOW OR ALONG A SHELF.

**1** Enlarge the pattern at the back of the book and trace one half of it onto construction paper (see Basic Techniques). Go over the tracing with a black pen so that it will show through easily. The design will fit onto a piece of letter paper folded in half lengthwise. Fold your paper in half and place the tracing along the inside fold. Trace the design onto your paper.

**2** Cut out the design, making the internal cuts first by gently piercing a hole and carefully cutting out each shape. Work on alternate ends of the cutting, top and bottom, so that the paper does not become flimsy from overhandling in one place.

**3** Finish by cutting a zigzag edge. Fold over the top and glue a length of string inside the fold for hanging.

## MATERIALS AND EQUIPMENT YOU WILL NEED

TRACING PAPER • PENCIL • CONSTRUCTION PAPER • BLACK FELT-TIP PEN • STRONG TRANSPARENT PAPER SUCH AS GLASSINE OR JAPANESE PAPER • SHARP SCISSORS OR CRAFT KNIFE • FINE STRING • GLUE STICK

# SHELF EDGING

PLAIN PAPER SHELF EDGINGS LIKE THIS ARE QUICKLY MADE AND CAN BE REPLACED EVERY NOW AND THEN TO GIVE A FRESH NEW LOOK. THIS IDEA IS USED ALL OVER THE WORLD, FROM THE FOLK ART PATTERNS OF NEW ENGLAND TO SOUTH AFRICA, WHERE COMIC STRIPS AND NEWSPAPERS ARE USED TO MAKE VIBRANT ZIGZAG BORDERS. THE PAPER USED HERE IS PLAIN NEWSPRINT PAPER, WHICH IS CHEAP AND A PLEASURE TO FOLD AND CUT. YOU CAN TRY PATTERNED PAPERS, TOO — GINGHAM PATTERNS LOOK GOOD ON KITCHEN SHELVES.

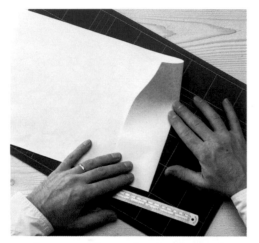

**1** Cut a strip of paper 9 inches deep and just a little bit longer than the length of the shelf. Make a fold 3 inches from one end of the paper.

**3** Trace your chosen pattern from the back of the book and transfer it to the folded paper (see Basic Techniques).

**5** Cut the edges of the pattern next, being careful not to tear the paper.

**2** Turn the paper strip over and repeat the fold. Continue in this way to make accordion folds along the whole length.

**4** Make the internal cuts first, using a craft knife and cutting mat.

**6** Unfold the paper and press. Fold in half lengthwise to fit over the shelf edges.

MATERIALS AND EQUIPMENT YOU WILL NEED

SCISSORS • PLAIN NEWSPRINT OR LINING PAPER • RULER • PENCIL • TRACING PAPER • CRAFT KNIFE • CUTTING MAT

# BOOKBINDING

THIS DESIGN IS INSPIRED BY A TRADITIONAL HAWAIIAN QUILT PATTERN. THE HAWAIIANS USE STRONGLY CONTRASTING COLORS TO APPLIQUÉ THE SAME PATTERN IN EACH QUILT BLOCK, THEN ATTACH THEM TO MAKE A DESIGN. THE PURPLE TISSUE PAPER USED HERE IS THIN ENOUGH TO CUT EASILY AND YET STRONG ENOUGH TO HOLD TOGETHER WHEN GLUED AND VARNISHED. THE RESULT IS A VIBRANT AND DYNAMIC PAPER THAT LOOKS STUNNING AS A BOOKBINDING.

1 Cut the tissue paper into 2-inch strips, then divide into 2-inch squares using a craft knife, metal ruler and cutting mat.

2 Stack four squares together and fold in half, then fold in half again to make a small square.

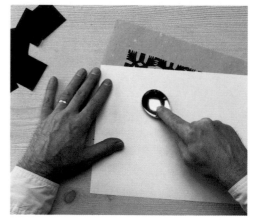

3 Photocopy the pattern from the back of the book. Cut the shapes freehand with the pattern in front of you for reference.

4 Open out the squares, then, using spray adhesive, mount them alongside each other to cover the background sheet of handmade paper.

5 Place tracing paper over the top and rub with the back of a spoon to make sure they are all stuck down evenly. Spray with two coats of matte varnish.

MATERIALS AND EQUIPMENT YOU WILL NEED

PURPLE TISSUE PAPER • CRAFT KNIFE • METAL RULER • CUTTING MAT • SPRAY ADHESIVE •
SHEET OF HANDMADE PAPER • TRACING PAPER • METAL SPOON • SPRAY MATTE VARNISH

# DESK ORGANIZER

MAKE YOUR MARK ON A STORE-BOUGHT DESK ORGANIZER WITH THESE SIMPLE BUT EFFECTIVE PAPERCUTS. THE PAPER STRIPS ARE TORN, FOLDED AND SNIPPED — THE SMALL AMOUNT OF TIME THIS TAKES WILL HELP TO MAKE YOUR WORK ENVIRONMENT JUST THAT MUCH MORE PERSONAL. THE PAPERS USED HERE ARE PACKING PAPER, CREAM WRITING PAPER AND THICK TRACING PAPER. AS WELL AS LOOKING GOOD, THE PAPERS PROVIDE AN INTERESTING TEXTURAL CONTRAST. YOU CAN DECORATE A FOLDER TO MATCH.

1 Measure the height of the desk organizer and divide it by three. Mark a strip of paper slightly narrower than this measurement, then place the ruler along the line and tear the paper so that you get a deckled edge. Place tracing paper over the top and rub with the back of a spoon to flatten the folds.

2 Cut another two strips in different papers. Fold each strip in half lengthwise.

3 Using a ruler and pencil, mark each strip at ½ inch intervals.

4 Draw a line 2 inches from the torn edges. Cut long rectangles up to this line and smaller ones in between. It should not look too measured and precise. The cream paper is cut in a similar way, with the longer rectangles a bit narrower and the shapes in between cut as small triangular notches. The tracing paper has triangular slits — one longer and wider than the other.

5 Apply a coat of spray adhesive to all the paper strips.

6 Stick the strips around the desk organizer one at a time.

MATERIALS AND EQUIPMENT YOU WILL NEED

DESK ORGANIZER • PENCIL • METAL RULER • ASSORTED PAPERS • TRACING PAPER • CUTTING MAT • SMALL, SHARP SCISSORS • SPRAY ADHESIVE

# PLACE MATS

MAKE A SET OF THESE STRIKING PLACE MATS AND YOU WILL ASK YOURSELF WHY YOU HAVE NEVER DONE IT BEFORE. ONE OF THE REASONS IS PROBABLY THAT A LAMINATING SERVICE IS NOT SOMETHING YOU USE UNTIL YOU HAVE A REASON — AND THEN YOU DISCOVER JUST HOW SIMPLE IT IS. A PAPERCUT WOULD NOT NOR- MALLY BE A PRACTICAL IDEA FOR A PLACE MAT, BUT ONCE IT HAS BEEN LAMINATED IT CAN BE WIPED CLEAN AND WILL LAST A LONG TIME. RED AND BLACK PROVIDE A STRIKING CONTRAST, BUT THE PAT- TERN CAN BE MADE IN ANY COLOR COMBINATION TO MATCH YOUR DINNER CHINA OR CURTAINS.

1 Trace the pattern from the back of the book onto a sheet of white paper and trim the edges.

3 Spray adhesive on the back of the pattern and stick it onto the red paper.

5 Carefully peel off the pattern, then open out and flatten the papercut.

2 Fold the red paper in half, then use the pattern to measure the size and trim the edges.

4 Cut through the pattern and the paper. Make the internal cuts first, starting in the middle and working outward, cutting the edges and along the fold last.

6 Spray adhesive on the back of the papercut and stick it onto the black paper. Cover it with a sheet of tracing paper and smooth with your hand to make sure that it has stuck down evenly. Take the mats to a print shop to be laminated.

MATERIALS AND EQUIPMENT YOU WILL NEED

TRACING PAPER • PENCIL • WHITE PAPER • CRAFT KNIFE • METAL RULER • CUTTING MAT • A SHEET EACH OF BLACK AND RED PAPER • SPRAY ADHESIVE

# 18TH-CENTURY ITALIAN PAPERCUT

Careful work with a steady hand is magnificently rewarded by the completion of this most intricate Italian design. It is made from a single sheet of thin black paper, folded in half and cut out with a craft knife. The photocopied pattern is temporarily glued to the black paper, which makes it easier to cut accurately because it is less flimsy. This papercut is very delicate and should be mounted on paper and framed.

1 Photocopy the pattern from the back of the book. Fold the piece of black paper in half.

2 Using the spray adhesive, stick the photo-copied pattern onto the folded paper.

4 Gently remove the pattern. Press the papercut flat by covering it with a sheet of tracing paper and rubbing with the back of a spoon.

3 Cut out the design carefully, working from the middle out toward the edges.

MATERIALS AND EQUIPMENT YOU WILL NEED

THIN BLACK PAPER (BETWEEN THE WEIGHT OF SUGAR PAPER AND TISSUE PAPER) • SPRAY ADHESIVE •

CRAFT KNIFE • CUTTING MAT • TRACING PAPER • METAL SPOON

# WHITE LACE SCHERENSCHNITTE

THE CUTTING OF VERY FINE FOLDED PAPER DESIGNS LIKE THIS ONE WAS A POPULAR PASTIME FOR LADIES IN THE 19TH CENTURY. THEY USED SMALL, SHARP EMBROIDERY SCISSORS TO CUT ELABORATE LOVE TOKENS FOR HUSBANDS OR SUITORS. MOST OF THE CUTTING HERE IS DONE WITH A SHARP CRAFT KNIFE, THEN A HOLE PUNCH COMPLETES THE DESIGN WITH PERFORATIONS TO GIVE A LACY EFFECT TO THE BORDER. LAID PAPER, WITH LINES RUNNING THROUGH IT, IS IDEAL FOR THIS DESIGN.

1 Photocopy the pattern from the back of the book. Fold the sheet of paper in half.

3 Using a craft knife and cutting mat, cut out the pattern. beginning in the center and working out toward the edges. Work slowly and carefully.

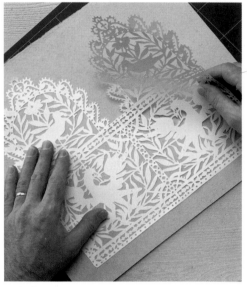

5 Open out the papercut and mount it onto a sheet of natural-colored handmade paper that has a  smooth enough texture not to distort the papercut.

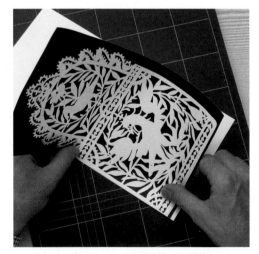

2 Spray adhesive onto the back of the pattern and position it on one half of the paper.

4 Remove the pattern. Using the finest setting on the hole punch, perforate the framework at regular intervals.

MATERIALS AND EQUIPMENT YOU WILL NEED
SPRAY ADHESIVE • SHEET OF WHITE LAID PAPER • CRAFT KNIFE • CUTTING MAT • REVOLVING HOLE PUNCH • SHEET OF NATURAL-COLORED HANDMADE PAPER

# STAR CLOCK

THE BOLD GRAPHIC STYLE OF THIS PAPER CLOCK FACE WILL SUIT ANY CONTEMPORARY ROOM AND WILL APPEAL TO ALL AGES. THE BASE IS MOUNTING BOARD, WITH LAYERS OF CUT PAPER FOR THE NUMERALS AND STARBURSTS. BATTERY-OPERATED CLOCK MOVE- MENTS ARE INEXPENSIVE, AND YOU CAN CHOOSE FROM A SELECTION OF HANDS — THESE VERY SIMPLE ONES SUIT THIS CLOCK FACE ESPECIALLY WELL BECAUSE THE RED SECOND HAND MATCHES THE NUMERALS. PRECISION CUTTING IS REQUIRED FOR THIS PROJECT.

1 Cut a 10-inch square of buff paper. Find the center of the square and use the compass to draw two circles, the first with a 4½-inch radius and the next with a 3¾-inch radius. Divide the circles into quarters vertically and horizontally, then use the compass to divide each quarter into thirds. This will give the positions for the 12 numerals.

2 Photocopy the numerals from the back of the book. Enlarge them if necessary, then cut them out using a craft knife, clear plastic ruler and cutting mat.

3 Using spray adhesive, mount each numeral in position around the clock face. The middle of each one should fall on the line that intersects the outer circle. Judge and adjust by eye. ▶

MATERIALS AND EQUIPMENT YOU WILL NEED

BUFF, RED, GRAY AND YELLOW PAPER • COMPASS • PENCIL • CRAFT KNIFE • CLEAR PLASTIC RULER • CUTTING MAT •
SPRAY ADHESIVE • GRAY MOUNTING BOARD • METAL RULER • BATTERY-OPERATED CLOCK MOVEMENT

4 Carefully cut out the numerals through both layers, then remove the paper.

5 Cut a 10¾-inch square of red paper and an 11½-inch square of gray mounting board using a craft knife, metal ruler and cutting mat.

6 Stick the buff and red paper in the middle of the gray mounting board.

7 Fold squares of gray and yellow paper in half and half again, then draw star patterns onto them, as shown (the yellow star should be slightly smaller than the gray star). Cut out both stars.

8 Position on the center of the clock face. Stick in place.

9 Cut a hole for the clock movement in the center and install it according to the manufacturer's instructions.

# VALENTINES

THE TRADITION OF MAKING PAPERCUT VALENTINES GOES BACK AT LEAST TWO HUNDRED YEARS. THERE IS A LOT OF PAPER CUTTING IN EUROPEAN FOLK ART, AND EMIGRANTS TOOK THEIR CUSTOMS TO AMERICA WHEN THEY SETTLED THERE. BOTH MEN AND WOMEN WOULD CUT ELABORATE LOVE TOKENS DECORATED WITH HEARTS, RIBBONS, BIRDS, FLOWERS AND STARS. WE HAVE USED ROUGH-TEXTURED HANDMADE PAPER FOR THE CARDS, THEN ADDED RED AND SILVER PAPERCUTS.

1 Fold the red paper in half, then fold the sheet of white paper around it. This will make it easier to cut accurately.

2 Trace one of the patterns from the back of the book onto the white paper.

3 Using a craft knife and cutting mat, make the internal cuts first, then those along the fold.

4 Turn the paper around so that you always cut at the most comfortable angle.

5 Fold the sheet of silver-coated packing paper in half and slide it into the fold of the papercut. Draw a half-heart shape around the outside of the papercut. ▶

## MATERIALS AND EQUIPMENT YOU WILL NEED

RED FIBROUS HANDMADE PAPER (FLECKED WITH PETALS OR LEAVES) • PLAIN WHITE PAPER • TRACING PAPER • PENCIL •
CRAFT KNIFE • CUTTING MAT • SILVER-COATED PACKING PAPER • METAL RULER • NATURAL-COLORED HANDMADE PAPER •
SPRAY ADHESIVE • TEXTURED SILVER FOIL PAPER (NOT ALUMINUM FOIL) • PINKING SHEARS

6 Using a metal ruler, tear a piece of natural-colored handmade paper a little bigger than the height of the silver heart.

8 Make the second card by folding the silver foil paper in half inside another sheet of plain white paper. Trace, then cut out the second shape with pinking shears.

7 Using spray adhesive, stick the heart and papercut onto the backing paper.

9 Cut a pattern along the fold, then open out and stick the foil cutout onto another torn backing sheet. Cut out small heart shapes to add more depth to the design.

# PICTURE FRAME

HERE IS A VERY SIMPLE BUT EFFECTIVE WAY TO CUSTOMIZE A SIMPLE WOODEN PICTURE FRAME. THE PATTERN OF DIAMONDS AND SQUARES HAS BEEN CUT FROM FIBROUS HANDMADE PAPER TO GIVE IT A "WOODY" APPEARANCE. THE PATTERN CAN BE PROTECTED BY A COAT OF CLEAR VARNISH, OR MADE TO LOOK LIKE MARQUETRY BY USING A TINTED VARNISH.

1 Place the frame on the handmade paper and draw around it with a pencil, inside and outside.

2 Using a craft knife, ruler and cutting mat, cut out just inside both lines, so that it is slightly smaller than the wooden frame.

4 Next, fold the longer side in half horizontally.

3 Fold the paper frame in half and then in half again.

## MATERIALS AND EQUIPMENT YOU WILL NEED

PLAIN WOODEN PICTURE FRAME • SHEET OF HANDMADE PAPER • PENCIL • CRAFT KNIFE • RULER •

CUTTING MAT • SPRAY ADHESIVE • CLEAR SPRAY VARNISH • TINTED VARNISH (OPTIONAL)

5 Draw triangles along the edge, leaving gaps in between and a square in the corner.

7 Cut out the inner triangles.

9 Apply a coat of spray adhesive and place the frame on top of the papercut.

6 Cut out the square and the outer triangles using a craft knife and cutting mat. Do one side, then unfold and refold it and draw and cut out the other side.

8 Unfold the papercut carefully and press it flat.

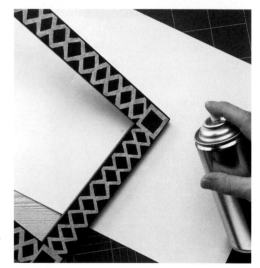

10 Make sure that the papercut is smoothly stuck down, then spray the frame with a clear varnish. If desired, you can add a tinted varnish at this stage.

# BOOKMARKS

THE IDEA FOR THESE UNUSUAL BOOKMARKS COMES FROM A COLLECTION OF AMERICAN FOLK ART THAT CONTAINS SIMILAR DESIGNS CUT FROM OLD LETTERS AND LEDGERS. CHILDREN WERE KEPT AMUSED FOR MANY HOURS WITH JUST A PAIR OF SCISSORS AND SOME PAPER. PAPER ITSELF WAS HARD TO COME BY, SO OLD LEDGERS, LETTERS AND HOUSEHOLD ACCOUNT BOOKS WERE RECYCLED AS PLAY MATERIALS. TO GET A SIMILAR EFFECT WE PHOTOCOPIED OLD DOCUMENTS ONTO COLORED PAPER.

1 Trim the colored paper to letter paper size so that it will fit in the photocopier.

2 Select the best part of your calligraphy and photocopy onto the colored paper.

3 Select the most suitable parts of your photocopied papers. Trim them to double the pattern size and fold in half.

4 Make photocopies of the patterns at the back of the book and cut them out.

5 Cut each pattern in half, spray the backs of the patterns lightly with spray adhesive and carefully stick them along the folds of the colored papers.

6 Using a craft knife, make all the inside cuts first.

MATERIALS AND EQUIPMENT YOU WILL NEED

COLORED LAID PAPER • OLD DOCUMENTS OR LEDGERS • CRAFT KNIFE • RULER • CUTTING MAT • SPRAY ADHESIVE

7 To finish the cutting, cut around the
outside edges.

8 Carefully peel off the pattern and open
out the papercut bookmarks.

# DOVE LAMPSHADE

Cutting a pattern out of a lampshade is an old idea, dating back to the days of pierced tin lanterns, which have also made a recent comeback. Candle shades would have had patterns cut out of them, or pricked out, to let the light shine through. This project is more about customizing a purchased shade rather than making one, and you can use any small paper shade — the vellum look used here is particularly suitable. If the lampshade is too stiff, you will find it hard to cut through. The dove pattern looks good during the day and even better once the lamp is lit.

1 Make a photocopy of the dove pattern from the back of the book, enlarging it to fit the size of your lampshade.

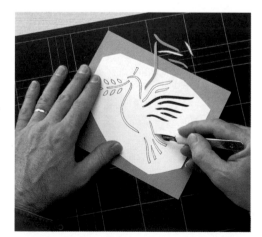

2 Using spray adhesive, mount the photocopy onto stiff paper. Cut out the design using a craft knife and cutting mat.

3 Peel off the photocopy to reveal the stencil.

4 Apply a light coating of spray adhesive, then tape the stencil onto the shade.

5 Carefully draw through the stencil to transfer the pattern onto the lampshade.

6 Hold the lampshade firmly with your spare hand and, keeping your fingers out of reach of the knife blade, cut out the pattern. When you cut, poke the point through first, then make sweeping cuts using the movement of your arm rather than just your wrist.

MATERIALS AND EQUIPMENT YOU WILL NEED

SMALL PAPER LAMPSHADE • SPRAY ADHESIVE • STIFF PAPER • CRAFT KNIFE • CUTTING MAT • MASKING TAPE • PENCIL

# DOILY

EVERYONE IS FAMILIAR WITH LACY WHITE PAPER DOILIES AND, THERE IS NO DOUBT ABOUT IT, THEY CAN TURN A HUMBLE PLATE OF COOKIES INTO A TEMPTING TEA-TIME TREAT! THIS IS MORE FUNKY THAN FRILLY. IT LOOKS GOOD IN TRADITIONAL WHITE, OR YOU CAN CUT DIFFERENT ONES FROM COLORED PAPER TO SUIT DIFFERENT FESTIVE OCCASIONS — ORANGE FOR HALLOWEEN, RED AND GREEN FOR CHRISTMAS, SILVER FOR A WEDDING OR BRIGHT MULTICOLORS FOR A BIRTHDAY PARTY.

1 Fold the paper diagonally to make a square. Cut off the excess, using a craft knife, ruler and cutting mat.

2 Find the center of the square by folding it diagonally and pinching.

3 Place the protractor on the center point and mark off a 36° angle. ▶

MATERIALS AND EQUIPMENT YOU WILL NEED
SHEET OF LETTER-SIZE PAPER • CRAFT KNIFE • RULER • CUTTING MAT • PROTRACTOR • PENCIL

4 Flip one side of the triangle over and fold along the 36° angle.

5 Fold the outer edge on top and crease firmly.

6 Now flip the paper over and repeat these folds, ending up with four layers of folds.

7 Using a pencil, draw a pattern on one side of the folded paper.

8 Using a craft knife and cutting mat, cut the internal cuts first, then the outside edge cuts.

9 Open out the papercut carefully and flatten out the doily.

# FRAKTUR-STYLE COLORED PAPERCUT

BEFORE THE DAYS OF THE PRINTING PRESS, CALLIGRAPHERS WOULD TRAVEL AROUND THE COUNTRY MAKING COMMEMORATIVE CERTIFICATES FOR BIRTHS, MARRIAGES AND DEATHS. THEY USED TRADITIONAL SYMBOLS AND PATTERNS TO DECORATE THE CERTIFICATES, THEN FILLED IN THE NAMES IN ELABORATE CALLIGRAPHY OR FRAKTUR WORK. THE PAPERCUT VERSION OF A FRAKTUR WAS MORE LIKELY TO BE MADE BY AN AMATEUR, TO BE GIVEN AS A GIFT OR TOKEN OF LOVE.

1 Photocopy the pattern from the back of the book. Fold the sheet of watercolor paper in half.

2 Spray adhesive onto the back of the pattern and stick it onto the folded paper. Carefully cut out the pattern using a craft knife and cutting mat. Make all the internal cuts first, then cut along the fold.

3 Remove the pattern carefully, open out, then cover with tracing paper and rub with the back of a spoon to flatten. ▶

MATERIALS AND EQUIPMENT YOU WILL NEED

SHEET OF WATERCOLOR PAPER, NOT TOO THICK • SPRAY ADHESIVE • CRAFT KNIFE • CUTTING MAT • TRACING PAPER • METAL SPOON • PAINT PALETTE •
GUM ARABIC • DISTILLED WATER • GREEN, YELLOW, ORANGE AND BLACK WATERCOLOR PAINTS • PAINTBRUSHES

4 Using a paint palette, prepare a watercolor medium for diluting the paints by mixing equal parts of gum arabic and distilled water.

7 Mix the orange in the same way and apply it.

5 Mix some green paint using the watercolor medium, and paint the green areas of the pattern.

8 Mix black in the same way and add the details with a fine brush.

6 Mix yellow paint in the same way and apply, following the illustration.

9 Let dry, then press flat under a heavy weight and mount for framing.

# JAM JAR COVERS

PRETTY PAPER CIRCLES LIKE THESE ARE PERFECT FOR DRESSING UP YOUR HOMEMADE JAMS AND CHUTNEYS TO GIVE AS PRESENTS OR TO SELL AT A FARMER'S MARKET. THEY MAKE AN ASSORTMENT OF UNMATCHING RECYCLED JARS INTO A SET THAT WILL STAND OUT FROM ALL THE REST WITH THEIR IMITATION LACE EDGINGS. THE PAPER USED HERE IS HANDMADE IN INDIA AND CONTAINS A LOT OF VEGETABLE FIBERS THAT ADD STRENGTH AND PREVENT IT FROM TEARING EASILY.

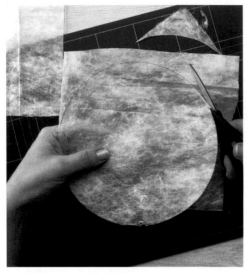

1 Cut out a circle of paper that is roughly twice the diameter of the jar lid.

2 Fold the circle of paper in half four times.

3 Lightly pencil in half-hearts on the edges and cut them out. Mark dotted hearts — one in the middle and two halves on either side — along the folded edges.

4 Place the folded paper on a hard surface and use the hole punch and hammer to tap out the dotted holes.

5 Using the small scissors, cut a scalloped edge by snipping out triangles between the bases of the hearts.

6 Unfold and flatten the cover. Place it over the jam jar and secure it with ribbon tied in a bow.

MATERIALS AND EQUIPMENT YOU WILL NEED

HANDMADE PAPER • SCISSORS — LARGE PAIR AND A SMALLER, POINTED PAIR • JAM JAR • PENCIL • SMALL HOLE PUNCH • SMALL HAMMER • RIBBON

# DECORATED ELEPHANTS

THIS PROJECT IS PART PAPER CUTTING AND PART PAPER SCULP-TURE. THERE IS SOMETHING REALLY MAGICAL ABOUT MAKING A FREE-STANDING ANIMAL OUT OF A FLAT SHEET OF PAPER AND THEN HAVING THE FUN OF DRESSING IT UP FOR A PROCESSION. A ROW OF THESE ELEPHANTS WOULD LOOK GREAT ALONG A SHELF OR MANTELPIECE, AND ONE ON ITS OWN WOULD MAKE A UNIQUE GREET-ING CARD. CHILDREN WILL ENJOY MAKING THE FANCY BLANKETS AND HEADDRESSES, AND ADDING SEQUINS, STARS AND FEATHERS.

1 Fold a sheet of colored letter size paper in half horizontally.

3 Place the paper on a cutting mat and cut out using a scalpel.

5 Holding the elephant firmly, push the head and shoulders toward each other to fold the head and ears back onto the body.

2 Trace, then transfer the elephant pattern from the back of the book, including the dotted and dashed fold lines. The dots indicate inward or valley folds, and the dashes indicate upward or mountain folds.

4 Make the folds by placing a small ruler along the line and using your thumbnail to fold and crease from the other side.

6 Fold the tail sideways and the tusks upward.

MATERIALS AND EQUIPMENT YOU WILL NEED

STIFF COLORED PAPER • PENCIL • CUTTING MAT • SCALPEL • SMALL METAL RULER • HANDMADE PAPER • DIFFERENT-COLORED AND TEXTURED PAPER, SUCH AS SCRAPS OF FOIL AND TISSUE PAPER • GLUE AND BRUSH • SEQUINS, FEATHERS AND STARS

7 Cut the under-blanket from a piece of natural-colored handmade paper, tearing the ends to make it look like frayed cloth.

9 Stick these to the elephant, then cut out a triangular headpiece and glue it in place firmly.

11 Glue a colored feather on top of the headpiece.

8 Cut several layers of different-colored and textured paper blankets with zig-zagged, scalloped or rounded edges.

10 Apply small dots of glue and stick on sequins for the eyes and blanket decoration.

12 Apply different-colored shiny star stickers to the elephant's body. When making a procession of elephants, you can change the order of colors and style of trimmings to add variety.

# PAPER FLOWERS

THIS JUST COULD BE THE PERFECT WAY TO SPEND A RAINY DAY. THE RESULTS WILL CERTAINLY BRIGHTEN UP A DULL CORNER. THE FLOWER PETALS ARE CUT FROM STIFF COLORED PAPER THAT HOLDS ITS SHAPE WELL, SO YOUR FLOWERS WILL NOT WILT IN THE VASE! CHOOSE YOUR FAVORITE COLOR COMBINATIONS AND MAKE THE FLOWERS AS BIG OR AS SMALL AS YOU LIKE — THE FLOWERS IN THIS ARRANGEMENT HAVE BEEN MADE TO ONE SIZE BUT YOU COULD PHOTOCOPY THE PATTERNS TO ANY SIZE.

1 Use the compass to draw 5-inch circles on colored paper. Cut them out with the larger scissors.

3 Draw on the petal shapes — one complete petal in the middle with a half petal on each side into the fold.

5 Draw a 3-inch circle for the center and cut out. Fold the circle as before, then trace and transfer a section of one of the patterns from the back of the book (see Basic Techniques).

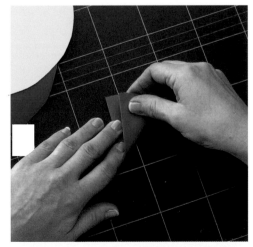

2 Fold each circle of colored paper in half three times.

4 Cut out around the petals. Open out the paper flowers.

6 Use the craft knife and cutting mat to make the small internal cuts.

MATERIALS AND EQUIPMENT YOU WILL NEED

COMPASS • PENCIL • STIFF COLORED PAPER • SCISSORS — LARGE PAIR AND A SMALLER, POINTED PAIR •
TRACING PAPER • CRAFT KNIFE • CUTTING MAT • GLUE AND BRUSH • WIRE • MASKING TAPE

**7** Use the small, pointed scissors to cut out the rest of the pattern.

**9** Twist the end of a piece of wire into a loop, then stick it to the back of each flower with masking tape. Arrange your bouquet!

**8** Apply a dab of glue to the center of each papercut and stick it in place.

# CYCLIST COLLAGE

IN POLAND THERE IS A TRADITION OF MAKING BRIGHTLY COLORED PAPERCUT PICTURES, USUALLY BASED ON BARNYARD SCENES OR RELIGIOUS THEMES. OUR CYCLIST IS NOT A TRADITIONAL SUBJECT, BUT THE INSPIRATION FOR THE PROJECT COMES FROM ALL THOSE WONDERFUL LIVELY IMAGES. COLORED PAPER IS SOLD IN PACKS OF DIFFERENT-COLORED SELF-ADHESIVE SQUARES, BUT WE HAVE CHOSEN TO USE GLUE FOR STICKING ON THE FRAGILE PIECES.

1 Make tracings of all the pattern pieces, except for the wheels, from the back of the book.

2 Transfer the tracings onto the colored paper (see Basic Techniques).

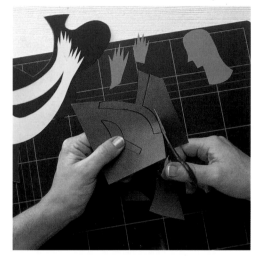

4 Cut out the parts of the bicycle, using small, sharp scissors.

▶

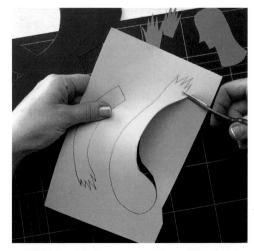

3 Cut out all the pieces of the cyclist using small, sharp scissors.

MATERIALS AND EQUIPMENT YOU WILL NEED

TRACING PAPER • PENCIL • COLORED ADHESIVE PAPER SQUARES • SMALL, SHARP SCISSORS • CRAFT KNIFE •
CUTTING MAT • WHITE GLUE AND BRUSH • BACKGROUND PAPER

5 Fold a piece of gray paper in half, and cut out the chain.

6 Draw two circles for the wheels, then fold in half three times.

7 Trace and transfer a section of each wheel pattern from the back of the book. Cut out the pattern. Unfold and flatten.

8 Draw and cut out the fine detailing for the cyclist's arms and legs. Fold up small circles of yellow paper and one green one, then cut out notches to make the wheel centers, bike light and cap badge.

9 Start to assemble the collage by sticking the detail pattern onto the cyclist's clothes. Then do the wheel spokes.

10 Arrange all the pieces on the background paper without sticking them down. When you are happy with the look of your picture, you can systematically stick each piece down. The right foot should be stuck down on top of the bicycle chain, last of all.

# SNOWFLAKES

WHEN YOU FOLD A CIRCLE OF PAPER A FEW TIMES AND SNIP OUT NOTCHES, SQUARES, SPIRALS AND TRIANGLES, AND UNFOLD IT, THE RESULTING PATTERN IS ALWAYS MUCH MORE COMPLEX THAN YOU EXPECT — EVEN THE SMALLEST NICK HAS A MATCHING HALF AND THE WHOLE SHAPE IS ECHOED ALL AROUND THE CIRCLE. THERE IS AN INFINITE NUMBER OF PATTERNS THAT YOU CAN MAKE BY COMBINING SIMPLE CUTS, AND BY USING SHINY REFLECTIVE PAPERS YOU CAN MAKE LIGHT-CATCHING HANGING DECORATIONS THAT LOOK LIKE LARGE SPARKLING SNOWFLAKES. THERE ARE PATTERNS TO TRACE IN THE BACK OF THE BOOK THAT WILL HELP YOU TO REPRODUCE THESE SNOWFLAKES, AND THEY WILL NO DOUBT LEAD YOU TO CREATE MANY MORE OF YOUR OWN DESIGNS.

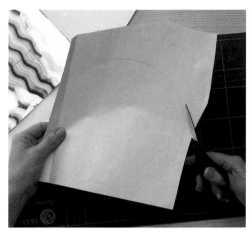

1 Draw a circle on the back of the reflective paper and cut it out with the larger scissors.

2 Fold the circle of reflective paper in half three times.

3 Photocopy the snowflake patterns from the back of the book, enlarging them to the size you want. Trace one of the segments.

4 Transfer the tracing onto the folded paper.

5 Use the small, sharp scissors to snip out the traced pattern shapes. Unfold the circle and flatten.

6 Do the same with the other papers and patterns, using the craft knife and cutting mat to make small, internal cuts. ▶

MATERIALS AND EQUIPMENT YOU WILL NEED

SELECTION OF REFLECTIVE SILVER, GOLD AND SPARKLING PAPERS • COMPASS • TRACING PAPER • PENCIL •
SCISSORS — LARGE PAIR AND A SMALLER, SHARP PAIR • CRAFT KNIFE • CUTTING MAT • GOLD THREAD

7 For the curved pattern, fold the circle in the usual way and cut the first part of the pattern with scissors.

9 Attach lengths of gold thread to hang up the snowflakes.

8 Now unfold once and fold in half the other way, then cut out triangular notches along the fold line.

# GREETING CARDS

E VERYONE ENJOYS RECEIVING A HANDMADE GREETING CARD, AND THESE ARE EYE-CATCHING AND GREAT FUN TO MAKE. THE SNOWFLAKE PATTERNS ARE MADE USING THREE DIFFERENT TYPES OF FOLD BEFORE CUTTING. THE WAY YOU FOLD THE PAPER AFFECTS THE NUMBER OF "SPOKES" YOU END UP WITH. THE PAPER USED HERE IS SELF-ADHESIVE GLOSSY CRAFT PAPER SOLD IN MULTICOLORED PACKAGES. IT IS GREAT FOR FOLDING AND CUTTING, BUT SPRAY ADHESIVE IS STILL BETTER FOR STICKING DOWN THE PAPERCUTS.

## THE FOUR FOLD

1 Fold a square of colored self-adhesive paper in half, then in half again to make a square.

2 Trace a section from one of the patterns at the back of the book and transfer it onto the paper square (see Basic Techniques).

3 Begin by cutting out all the shapes along the fold lines, using a craft knife and cutting mat.

MATERIALS AND EQUIPMENT YOU WILL NEED
GLOSSY COLORED SELF-ADHESIVE PAPER SQUARES • TRACING PAPER • PENCIL • CRAFT KNIFE • CUTTING MAT • SPRAY ADHESIVE •
STIFF COLORED CARDBOARD • 60/30° TRIANGLE • ENVELOPES TO FIT CARDS

4 Next, make all the internal cuts (see Basic Techniques).

5 Finish the papercut by cutting the pattern along the edges.

6 Open up the papercut and glue it onto a piece of contrasting colored cardboard.

## THE EIGHT FOLD

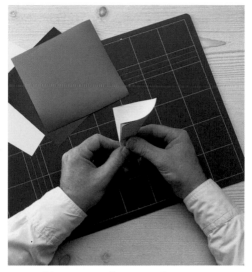

7 Fold a square of paper in the same way as for the four fold, then fold diagonally into a triangle.

8 Trace a quarter section of one of the patterns from the back of the book and transfer the tracing. Cut out the shapes in the same order as before.

## THE SIX FOLD

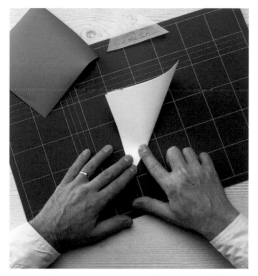

9 Fold the square diagonally once. Fold it in half again but only press down to mark the center point, then unfold it again.

10 Place the triangle at the center point along the fold to get a 60° fold. Hold it firmly and fold the paper up around it, marking the crease with your thumbnail.

▶

**11** Flip the paper over and flatten it, then fold the other side over to make a symmetrical tulip shape.

**12** Transfer the traced pattern onto this and cut out in the same order as before.

# SILHOUETTE

**B**EFORE THE CAMERA WAS INVENTED, PEOPLE WHO COULD NOT AFFORD TO HAVE A PORTRAIT PAINTED WOULD USE THE SERVICES OF THE SILHOUETTE ARTIST. THE SUBJECT WOULD SIT BY A SCREEN WITH A LIGHT TO PROJECT THE SHADOW OF THEIR PROFILE, OR THE SKILLED ARTIST MIGHT CUT FREEHAND JUST FROM LOOKING AT HIS SUBJECT. OUR METHOD PRODUCES A VERY ACCURATE LIKENESS USING ALL THE TRICKS OF MODERN TECHNOLOGY TO MAKE A CHARMING, OLD-FASHIONED PORTRAIT.

1 Enlarge the photograph on a photocopier to fit your mount.

2 Select the best photocopy. Use a pencil to draw in the "bust" shape that is typical on old silhouettes.

3 Using a craft knife and cutting mat, cut very carefully around the face and cut a bit extra around the hair. You may find it easier to cut the profile with small, sharp scissors — it is a personal preference.

4 Turn the cutout over and color it with a black marker. Be careful not to overwork the edges as every dent will show. ▶

MATERIALS AND EQUIPMENT YOU WILL NEED

PROFILE PHOTOGRAPH • OVAL PHOTO MOUNT • PENCIL • CRAFT KNIFE OR SMALL, SHARP SCISSORS •

CUTTING MAT • BLACK PERMANENT INK MARKER • SPRAY ADHESIVE • CREAM PAPER • RED PAPER • PINKING SHEARS • GLUE AND BRUSH

5 Add the finishing touches to the edges of the hair — this is where the extra allowance is useful. Spray the back of the profile with adhesive and position it in the center of the cream paper.

6 To make the decorated border, place the oval mount on the back of a sheet of red paper and draw around the inside edge.

7 Cut out the red paper and fold it in quarters.

8 Cut out the shape inside the line using pinking shears.

9 Glue the red paper mount onto the cream paper.

10 Leave the silhouette as it is or add the black photo mount on top.

# CAKE TIN

THE RECIPE HERE IS QUITE SIMPLE — TAKE ONE PLAIN TIN, DO SOME CLEVER SNIPPING AND STICKING AND PRODUCE A MASTERPIECE! THE SECRET OF SUCCESS LIES IN THE STRONG CONTRAST BETWEEN THE TWO COLORS. DO NOT DESPAIR IF YOU CANNOT FIND A SHINY NEW TIN; JUST SPRAY PAINT AN OLD ONE AND GIVE IT A NEW LEASE ON LIFE. USE THE BEST-QUALITY TISSUE PAPER THAT IS SOLD IN ART AND HOBBY STORES BECAUSE IT IS MUCH STRONGER AND COMES IN A RANGE OF VIBRANT COLORS.

1 Cut a strip of tissue paper to fit around the tin — use the tin as a guide.

2 Fold the strip in half three times, firming each crease as you go.

3 Photocopy the patterns for this project from the back of the book. Keep the pattern of the figures in front of you and draw onto the tissue paper — tracing does not really suit fine paper, so rely on observation.

4 Cut out the pattern using small, pointed scissors and turning the paper to meet them, not the other way around.

5 Place the lid on the tissue paper and draw around it. ▶

MATERIALS AND EQUIPMENT YOU WILL NEED

SCISSORS — LARGE PAIR AND A SMALLER, POINTED PAIR • BRIGHT BLUE TISSUE PAPER • PLAIN CAKE TIN WITH LID • PENCIL • SPRAY ADHESIVE • CLEAR MATTE VARNISH • SOFT PAINTBRUSH

6 Cut out the circle and fold it in half three times.

8 Unfold the circle, and then, using spray adhesive, mount it on the lid. Apply at least one coat of clear varnish with a soft brush to protect the surface and allow it to be wiped clean.

7 Again keeping the pattern for the lid alongside for reference, draw out the pattern, then cut it out.

9 Using spray adhesive, stick the papercut strip around the side of the tin. Seal this with varnish and allow plenty of drying time before placing the lid on the tin.

# TEMPLATES

THESE ARE THE PATTERNS YOU WILL NEED FOR THE PROJECTS. THEY ARE PRESENTED IN TWO DIFFERENT STYLES. FIRST OF ALL, THERE ARE SOME FOR WHICH THE WHOLE DESIGN IS GIVEN AND YOU EITHER HAVE TO TRACE THE WHOLE DESIGN, OR JUST A SECTION, USUALLY HALF OR A QUARTER, AND TRANSFER IT ONTO YOUR CHOSEN PAPER. SECONDLY, THERE ARE SOME FOR WHICH ONLY THE SECTION YOU HAVE TO TRACE IS GIVEN. FOLLOW THE STEPS FOR EACH PROJECT AND THEY WILL TELL YOU WHICH PART TO TRACE.

### DECORATED LAMPSHADE, PP. 20–21

### PAPER CAFÉ CURTAIN, PP. 26–27

### MEXICAN PAPERCUT BUNTING, PP. 28–29

SHELF EDGING, PP. 30–31

PLACE MAT, PP. 36–37

18TH-CENTURY ITALIAN PAPERCUT, PP. 38–39

WHITE LACE SCHERENSCHNITTE, PP. 40–41

STAR CLOCK, PP. 42–44

1 2 3 4
5 6 7 8
9 10
11 12

BOOKBINDING, PP. 32–33

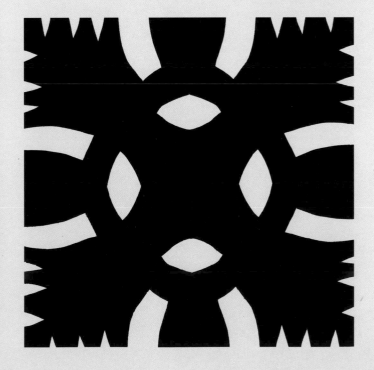

BOOKMARKS, PP. 51–53

VALENTINES, PP. 45–47

DOVE LAMPSHADE, PP. 54–55

FRAKTUR-STYLE COLORED PAPERCUT, PP. 59–61

DECORATED ELEPHANTS, PP. 64–66

PAPER FLOWERS, PP. 67–69

CYCLIST COLLAGE, PP. 70–72

CAKE TIN, PP. 83–85

SNOWFLAKES, PP. 73–75

GREETING CARDS, PP. 76–79

# SUPPLIERS

For many of the projects in this book you can use paper that you have on hand. If you want to buy paper, the range available today is enormous. There are specialty stores, and most craft and hobby stores stock a good collection. Listed here are a few addresses.

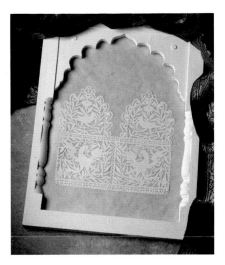

The Art Store
935 Erie Blvd. E.
Syracuse, NY 13210
USA
Tel (315) 474-1000

Joe Kubert Art & Graphic Supply
37A Myrtle Ave.
Dover, NJ 07801
USA
Tel (201) 328-3266

Zimmerman's
2884 35th St. N.
St. Petersburg, FL 33713
USA
Tel (813) 526-4880

Dick Blick
P.O. Box 1267
Galesburg, IL 61402
USA
Tel (309) 343-6181

National Artcraft Co.
23456 Mercantile Rd.
Beachwood, OH 44122
USA
Tel (216) 963-6011

Papersource Inc.
730 N Franklin Suite 111
Chicago, IL 60610
USA
Tel: (312) 337 0798

Creative Craft House
897 San Jose Circle, HC 62
P.O. Box 7810
Bullhead City, AZ 86430
USA
Tel (520) 754-3300

S & S Arts & Crafts
P.O. Box 513
Colchester, CT 06415
USA
Tel (800) 243-9232,
Dept. 2007

Kate's Paper ie
8 West 13th Street
New York
NY 10011
USA
Tel: (212) 941 9816

# ACKNOWLEDGMENTS

The authors and publishers would like to thank the following people who contributed projects to the book: Penny Boylan, pages 20, 22 and 26; Madhu and Ray McChrystal, 34, 64, 67, 71 and 83. They would also like to thank the Abby Aldrich Rockefeller Folk Art Center, Williamsburg, VA, for the loan of the pictures on pages 9b and 10, and Mexique, 67 Sheen Lane, East Sheen, London SW14 8AD, for the loan of the Mexican papercuts.

The following stores kindly lent materials as props for the photography: The Holding Company, 243–245 Kings Road, London SW3, 0171 352 7495; V.V. Rouleaux, 10 Symons Street, London SW3, 0171 730 3125; The Shaker Shop, 322 Kings Road, London SW3, 0171 352 3918; Yound & D. Ltd, Beckhaven House, 9 Gilbert Road, London SE1, 0171 820 9403; Paperchase, 213 Tottenham Court Road, London W1P 9AF, 0171 734 9494.

## AUTHORS' ACKNOWLEDGMENTS

The authors would like to thank their lovely new friend, Lorne Ormond, for her enthusiasm in searching out original ideas for this book. Thanks also to Ray and Madhu, who are a pleasure to work with and a joy to know, and Peter Williams for his wonderful photography.

# INDEX